CYBER CRIME PROTECTION FOR BEGINNERS

THE BATTLE AGAINST CYBER CRIME IN THE 21ST CENTURY

FELIX TAIWO

Cybercrime Protection for Beginners

The Battle Against Cyber Crime in the 21st Century

Felix Taiwo

Cybercrime Protection for Beginners

The Battle Against Cyber Crime in the 21st Century

Felix Taiwo

Copyright ©2012

Copyright Notice

Legal Notice

Table of Contents

ABOUT THE AUTHOR

Felix A Taiwo is the Director/Principal of London College of Science and Technology Limited (London).

He holds LLM in Corporate Law and Strategy and MSc in Forensic Accounting, both from Sheffield Hallam University. He gained Law experience from Olubi Solicitors in London. He also holds Postgraduate Certificate in Education from University of Greenwich, and BSc Accounting from Greenwich School of Management.

He has spent a lot of time investigating reasons for computer viruses, defences, security, governance, information security and computer forensics. As an educator, he has taught courses in digital forensics for 3 years. He was the Managing Director of M and T Systems Software LTD for 8 years.

He is a member of the following bodies: Certified Fraud Examiner, British Computer Society, and Forensic Certified Public Accountant. He is happily married to Pastor (Mrs) Elizabeth Adetoun Taiwo and blessed with children.

x

Introduction

The widespread use of information and communication technology (ICT) has created a global platform for the exchange of ideas. It has also created boundless opportunities for fraud and deception.

Cybercrime is one of the most widespread criminal practices around the globe, whether in the form of violation of company policies, fraud, crime, child pornography, or terrorism. It is therefore paramount that organisations, industries, and individuals raise their game to combat these threats.

This is an issue of global importance as researchers, government officials, company executives and law enforcement agencies all over the world are struggling to cope with cybercrime. The significance of this issue has been highlighted in national and international media. According to a UK newspaper the Daily metro of 25th of September 2010, "Bank Customers are being urged to be more vigilant than ever after a surge in identity fraud. Almost 300 people a day fell victim to the crime in the first half of the year"[i]

Furthermore, this widely read UK newspaper stresses:

"It has emerged that criminal gangs in Eastern Europe are targeting British online bank customers, using computer viruses to hack into bank systems and steal from customers' accounts."

It is apparent from above that fraudsters are often one giant step ahead. Jemma Smith of UK payments, which represents the payments industry, confirms this by saying "fraudsters are often one step ahead. However, customers can take steps to protect themselves and reduce the risks."[ii]

The aim of this book is to explore some strategies to win the battle against cybercrime.

Chapter One

What is Cybercrime?

Cybercrime is criminal activity done using computers and the internet. These include anything from downloading illegal music files to stealing millions of pounds from online bank accounts. Cybercrime also includes non-monetary offenses, such as creating and distributing viruses on other computers and internet

Fraud against online bank customers surged 14 per cent in 2010 and it is costing banks almost £60 million a year. UK payments blame a rise in phishing attacks on criminals who use malware to hack into customers' account. Malware can be installed on a computer without the owner's knowledge, typically when they click on an email link or download software.[iii]

Phishing

This is when fraudsters send a fake email purporting to be from a bank or other institution hoping to trick consumers into disclosing information such as passwords and Personal Identification Numbers (PIN) through a bogus website.

Trojan Virus

Thousands of online banking customers have accounts emptied by one of the most dangerous Trojan viruses ever created.[iv] These Trojan viruses were created by the cyber criminals who raided the accounts of thousands of British internet bank customers in one of the most sophisticated attacks of its kind.[v]

The fraudsters used a malicious computer programme that hides inside computers to steal confidential passwords and account details from people. The internet security experts M86, who uncovered the scam, estimated that at least £675,000 has been illegally transferred from the UK. The new Trojan virus can empty bank accounts without their owners knowing about the theft as it shows them fake statements.

Solution to Trojan and Phishing

Make sure your anti-virus software is up to date.

Keep firewalls set to the highest level.

Never open an email attachment that ends in .exe. It is an 'executable' file and it can do what it likes in your system.

The latest Trojan virus which is called Zeus V3 hides inside adverts on legitimate websites. Once installed on your computer, the programme waits until the user visits their online bank and then secretly records their account details and passwords. It will then use this information to transfer any amount to other accounts.

Another dangerous virus is production of a software code known as malware, which can harm computers and steal users' passwords. The use of this virus reached a new high in the first six months of 2010. Total malware production continued to increase and 10 million new pieces of malicious codes were catalogued to be used by criminals. There were millions of viruses and other malicious software. People should take basic measures to protect themselves from virus attacks.

According to the report from the Daily Mail of August 2010, £59.7 million[vi] was stolen in online banking fraud, while another £440 million was lost to credit card fraud.

Warning:

Sometimes suddenly an alarm email may pop up into your mail saying your account is about to be shut down unless you confirm all your details with them. Many people fall victim to 'Phishing' when they receive hoax emails appearing to have been sent from a legitimate source. You need to be careful when clicking on your email, especially when you do not know where it comes from.

Beware of Identity crime:

"In the Metro newspaper of 18th of October, 2010 a Metro Reporter Tariq Tahir"[vii] says the following:

Nearly 2 million people fall victim to identity fraud a year, costing the country £2.7billion a year. Each victim is stung for an average of £1000 in credit or benefits, according to a report by the National Fraud Authority. Their stolen identities are also used to commit other crimes, ranging from evading police to people trafficking and terrorism.

In the most serious cases, it can take victims more than 200 hours equivalent of a year's annual leave to resolve the problems caused by identity fraud. National Fraud Authority executive Bernard Herdan said the crime often has a devastating impact on its victims.

Chapter Two

Computer viruses

Computer virus is a kind of malicious software written intentionally to enter a computer without the user's permission or knowledge. It has the ability to replicate itself, thus continuing to spread. Some viruses do little, but replicated viruses can cause severe harm or adversely affect program and performance of the system. A virus should never be assumed harmless and left on a system.

There are different types of computer viruses that can damage your system. Most common types of viruses are mentioned below:

Resident Viruses

These types of viruses are permanent and dwell in the RAM memory. From there they can overcome and interrupt all of the operations executed by the system: corrupting files and programs that opened, closed, copied, renamed. Examples include: Randex, CMJ, Meve and MrKlunky.

Direct Action Viruses

The main purpose of these viruses is to replicate and take action when it is executed. When a specific condition is met, the virus will go into action and infect files in the directory or folder that it is, in the directories that are specified in the AUTOEXEC.BAT file PATH. This batch file is always located in the root directory of the hard disk and carries out certain operations when the computer is booted.

Overwrite Viruses

Viruses of this kind are characterised by the fact that they delete the information contained in the files that they infect, rendering them partially or totally useless once they have been infected. The only way to clean a file infected by an overwrite virus is to delete the file completely, thus losing the original content. Examples of overwrite viruses include: Way, TrjReboot, Trivial. 88.D.

Boot Viruses

These viruses affect the boot sector of a floppy or hard disk. This is a crucial part of a disk, in which information on the disk itself is stored together with a program that makes it possible to boot (start) the computer from the disk. The best way of avoiding boot viruses is to ensure that floppy disks are write protected and never start your computer with an unknown floppy disk in the disk drive. Examples of boot viruses include: Poly boot B, Anti EXE.

Macro Viruses

Macro viruses infect files that are created using certain applications or programs that contain macros. These mini-programs make it possible to automate series of operations so that they are performed as a single action, thereby saving the user from having to carry them out one by one. Examples of macro viruses include: Relax, MelissaA, Bablas, 097M/ Y2K.

Directory Viruses

Directory viruses change the paths that indicate the location of a file. By executing a program (file with the extension .EXE or .Com) which has been infected by a virus, you are unknowingly running the virus program, while the original file and program have been previously moved by the virus. Once infected, it becomes impossible to locate the original files.

Polymorphic Viruses

Polymorphic viruses encrypt or encode themselves in a different way using different algorithms and encryption keys every time they infect a system. This makes it impossible for anti-viruses to find them using string or signature searches (because they are different in each encryption) and also enables them to create a large number of copies of themselves. Examples include: Elkem, Marburg, Satan Bug and Tuareg.

File Infectors

This type of virus infects programs or executable files (files with an .EXE or Com.extension). When one of these programs is run, directly or indirectly, the virus is activated, producing the damaging effects it is programmed to carry out. The majority of existing viruses belong to this category, and can be classified depending on the actions that they carry out.

Companion Viruses

Companion viruses can be considered file infector viruses like resident or direct action types. They are known as companion viruses because once they get into the system they accompany the other files that already exist. In other words, to carry out their infection routines, companion viruses can wait in memory until a program is run (resident viruses) or act immediately by making copies of themselves (direct action viruses). Examples include: Stator, Asimor, 1539, and Terrax 1069.

FAT Viruses

This file allocation table or FAT is the part of a disk used to connect information and is a vital part of the normal functioning of the computer. This type of virus attack can be especially dangerous, as it prevents access to certain sections of the disk where important files are stored. Damage caused can result in information losses from individual files or even entire directories.

Chapter Three

Malicious codes:

Definition - What does Malicious Code mean?

"Malicious code is code causing damage to a computer or system. It is code not easily or solely controlled through the use of anti-virus tools. Malicious code can either activate itself or be like a virus requiring a user to perform an action, such as clicking on something or opening an email attachment." [1]

Worms

A worm is a program very similar to a virus, it has the ability to self-replicate, and can lead to negative effects on your system and most importantly they are detected and eliminated by anti-viruses. Examples of worms include: PSWBugbear B, Lovgate F. Trile C, Sobig. D, Mapson.

Trojans or Trojan Horses

Another unsavoury breeds of malicious code are called Trojans or Trojan horses, which unlike

---

[1] By Cory Janssen: www.techopedia.com

viruses do not reproduce by infecting other files, nor do they self- replicate like worms.

Logic Bombs

They are not considered viruses because they do not replicate. They are not even programs in their own right but rather camouflaged segments of other programs. Their objective is to destroy data on the computer once certain conditions have been met. Logic bombs go undetected until launched, and the results can be destructive.

Spyware

It is transmitted information gathered from a computer, such as bank details. Example: Key logging software records anything entered using the keyboard, such as passwords.

Melissa:

Once infected with this virus, a computer would automatically send copies of a word document to the first fifty names in the user's Microsoft outlook email address book. Once opened by the recipients, the process would be repeated.

Sasser:

This virus achieves its effects through exploiting a weakness in the windows operating system. It is capable of infecting any computer which is connected to the internet without the owner needing to take any further action, such as opening an email attachment.

Chapter Four

Solution to computer viruses

It is necessary to ensure that a desktop firewall is in place. A firewall is software or hardware that acts as a fitter between your computer or network and the internet. Using a firewall prevents unauthorised access to your computer and is designed to stop worms.

Using up to-date antivirus Software:

Antivirus software will check your computer for viruses and alerts you of any virus. It is important to keep this software up to date, as new viruses are being created all the time.

Use Strong Passwords:

Many websites use passwords to protect your identity. If passwords get into the wrong hands or are easy to guess, your personal details will be easily accessible. Good passwords should

- Never be shared, including with helping staff or written down.
- Be at least seven characters long.

- Be a mixture of lower and upper case letters, numbers and other keyboard characters.
- Be changed regularly every three months. This is a good guide.
- Not be the same on all the websites you use.

It is highly advisable to avoid disclosing personal information as much as possible. It is also a protective measure to open email attachments only from people you know. Be careful about sharing files and downloading software, as these can easily spread viruses and hide spyware.

Internet Terms and Language

There is a lot of information available about the dangers of the internet. The language can be confusing if you are not familiar with it. This guide will help you understand the basic terms used when talking about being online.

The internet lets users chat with friends and family in interactive virtual communities. These communities are increasingly popular with children because they enable them to communicate in real time. Real time means their contributions or posts are displayed immediately, for example in an online chat. However, not all virtual communities will be moderated or supervised.

Examples of sites children may use to chat with others online: Chat rooms are virtual rooms where users can talk with each other by typing, either one-on-one or involving a number of people.

Forums

Forums are online discussion groups. These discussions can take place in real time or over a longer period (users can continue to add comments)

Blogs

Blogs are like online diaries. The blogger publishes comments and discussions and readers can also add their views (blog is short for web log)

Instant messaging services

Instant messaging (IM) services (which look like small pop-up windows) let users see when people are online or the lists of their friends when they are online and can send messages to them. Yahoo messenger is an example of an instant messaging service

Social Networking Site

Social networking sites are online communities of people who have a number of different ways of communicating with each other.

Different Types of Social Networks

"Many social networks can be broken up into many categories and most networks fall into more than one category. Knowing what category a network is classed as is vital to plan out a social media management campaign and also to have a successful return on your social media efforts.

There are seven main types of social networks and every social service can be categorised into at least one of these: Blogs, Social networking services, Social media sharing, Social bookmarking, Social news services, Location based networking and Community building services.

Blogs
Blogs were one of the first forms of social media and have really evolved. Blogs are designed to allow easy content posting, and also easy commenting and sharing. Examples of blogging services are: WordPress, Type Pad and Blogger.

Social Networking Services
Social Networking Services were originally created for the sole purpose of two way communication and

content sharing, e.g. videos, picture and information. Even with this category, there are three sub categories: Full networks (Facebook/Google +), Micro blogging (Twitter/Plurk) and Professional Networks (Linkedin/Xing).

Social Media Sharing Services

Social media sharing services are based around posting content such as videos and pictures, and sharing the content and also commenting on it. There are three types of these networks, video (YouTube/Vimeo), Photos (Flickr/Picasa), Audio (Podcast Alley).

Users of social bookmarking services can bookmark their favourite pages for other users of that network to see and enjoy. Recommendation sites (Stumble Upon/Delicious), Social Shopping (Kaboodle/This Next).

Social News Services

Users of social news services can favourite news for the rest of the network to see, these articles are usually voted on in some way. Examples of these services are Digg and Reddit.

Location Based Networking

Location based networking is something users have to help bring them closer together and explore their local area. Examples of this are Foursquare, Gowalla and Loopt.

Community Building Services
Community building services are mostly forum like networks such as Yahoo!, and Google Groups. These networks can be very niche."[2]

Online grooming: It is when a suspected paedophile behaves in a way that suggests they are trying to contact children for illegal purposes. Grooming offenders pretend to be children themselves to start online conversations with children. They might then try to continue the relationship in personal conversations on mobile phones (sometimes known as whispering).

Once they have established some trust, the offender may try to organise a meeting with the child. This may take weeks, months, or even years. As part of the grooming process, the offender might also try to exploit by sending them indecent pictures or pornographic images. This might be by email or sometimes by using a webcam (a camera connected to a computer, which can produce pictures.

---

[2] www.seo-positive.co.uk

The offender may use blackmail to persuade the child to do something they do not want to do.

Solution

By blocking access to unsupervised chat rooms, blogs and forums, you can help your child stop communicating with people they do not know. Parents should make sure that their children know the online dangers. Making children aware of the online dangers is just like teaching them what they should know about life safety. The internet can be fun and useful but you and your children need to know the risks too. It is vital your child knows that not everyone on the internet is who they claim to be.

Chapter Five

Online fraud and financial transactions

Definition of online fraud

"Online or internet fraud can be defined as any type of intentional deception that uses the Internet. It includes fraud that occurs in chat rooms, message boards, web sites and through e-mail. It occurs in the form of deceitful solicitations and fraudulent transactions."[3]

Counterfeit fraud (skimming), lost or stolen cards, identity fraud, Cash-point Fraud, facebook impersonation, postal interceptions, and many more.

Skimming

Skimming is when someone copies the data from your card's magnetic strip onto another card without your knowledge. It can happen anywhere – cash machines, shops, bars, restaurants and petrol stations. Always make sure you can see your card when you are making a transaction.

---

[3] www.ehow.co.uk

Lost or Stolen Cards:

It is easy to lose your card or have it stolen. You could drop it in a shop when you take something else out of your pocket, or you could put it down and forget to pick it up.

Identity Fraud

If personal details like your address, passport number and national insurance number or social security number are stolen they can be used to set up online accounts or to apply for credit cards; and apply for benefits in your name without you knowing.

Criminals may try to get your credit card details by sending emails that appear to be from a reputable online organisation like a bank or a credit card company. They may encourage you to enter your credit card details or password on a fake website.

Credit Card Fraud

"Credit card and debit card fraud is costing the industry more than £290 million a year. The reason was mainly due to counterfeiting cards, which more than doubled during 2000, as well as a 94% rise in fraud using stolen credit card details to pay for things over the telephone or internet, according to the association for payment clearing services (APACS)"[viii].

Facebook Impersonation

The crime one should most worry about is facebook impersonation. A criminal who hacks into your facebook account can learn and steal a great amount of information about you. He or she can gain trusted access to friends and family. There have been many stories that show facebook friends can easily be tricked into sending money.

Postal Interceptions

If you are expecting a new card or cheque book through the post and it does not arrive, call your bank immediately or report to your local post office.

Email fraud

Fraudulent email activity is increasing. These emails may appear to be from legitimate companies that you do business with such as your bank, an online auction site, or your internet service provider. You are often asked to validate or confirm your personal information or opening an attachment. These messages can contain viruses, known as 'Trojan horse' programs, designed to record your keystrokes. These emails can also direct you to counterfeit web sites that appear to be genuine.

Avoiding Online Financial Fraud

Buying and selling online is just as safe as ordering goods over the phone, but you should be aware that dishonest people may try to convince you to give them your card or personal details.

How do you keep your financial details safe? Before you buy anything online make a note of the address of the company that you are buying from. This should include details of the telephone and/or fax number. Never rely on just an email address.

It is of utmost necessity that you use secure sites always. These sites have 'https' in front of the web address which indicates that the company has been independently checked to make sure they are who they say they are. A yellow padlock symbol will appear in the browser window to show the payment process is secure when buying online.

Other things to bear in mind should include the following:

1. Check the site's privacy and returns policy.
2. Print out a copy of your order and any acknowledgement you receive.
3. Check your bank statement carefully against anything you buy online.
4. Keep your password secure.

You may be a victim of internet fraud if any or some of the following happen:

1. If you have paid for an item online and it does not arrive.
2. You sell something online and you don't receive payment.
3. The item you received doesn't match the original description you were given.
4. If you have a problem with an item bought or sold using an auction site, like eBay, check with them to see if they can do anything about it.
5. If you paid for goods using a credit card and the goods did not arrive, you can ask the credit card company to investigate.

6. If you used an online payment service, check if you are covered by a fraud protection scheme on the service website.

You will protect yourself by keeping in mind that the internet provides criminals with an easy way to contact thousands of people at a time. Examples include emails offering the chance to take part in money making scheme, or claiming you are the winner of a prize draw.

You can avoid being a victim of internet fraud by doing the following:

1. Remember if something sounds too good to be true, it is usually better to seek independent financial advice before making investments.
2. Only do business with companies that you recognise or know through recommendation by someone you trust.
3. Do not judge a company on how professional its website may look. If in any doubt, you can check if a company is genuine by looking at its profile on Companies House or Financial Services Authority (FSA) websites or other associated public services..

Chapter Six

Tips on protecting yourself against cybercrime

1. Never tell anyone either your PIN or password or write it down.
2. Never give anyone your card and tell them your PIN.
3. Keep your information up to date, if you change your address, inform your bank immediately.
4. Tell your bank whenever you are going abroad so as to inform you of a strange transaction.
5. Shred any sensitive information, shred all financial statements, offer of loans and credit cards, account details or anything else that could be used to impersonate you before binning them. Thieves go through rubbish to see if there is anything useful for them. This is known as bin raiding.
6. Check your statements carefully, go through your credit card and bank statements every month. Unexpected entries can be the first indication that somebody is stealing your money.
7. Learning to check your credit report is an effective tool in the fight against Identity

fraud. It gives you a snapshot of your borrowings and repayment history. You can easily spot unfamiliar accounts and suspicious balances.

8. Limit your social networking. It is dangerous to include basic information such as your full name and date of birth, pets or children's names and nicknames in your profile. Do not do it. These are the kind of details that you probably use for your passwords, never included such in your profile.

9. Do not carry your passport, driving licence or credit cards around unless you know you will need them, and never write down your PINs and your passwords. If your bag or wallet is stolen, you could be handing the thieves your identity.

10. Report thefts always to the police, your bank, and credit card issuers.

11. Keep an eye on your mails, and if your mail goes missing tell the post office immediately, someone may be intercepting it. Be careful when you move house. Make sure to use the in-country mail redirection service to forward your post to your new

address for at least a year. In the UK, it is the Royal mail.

12. Register to vote at your current address. Lenders use the electoral roll to check that you live where you say you reside. If you are not registered, a criminal could register you at another address.

13. Never reply to emails and cold callers asking for details such as PINS, passwords and account numbers, and do not fill in your details on any unfamiliar email or website.

14. Keep on checking your credit report. You need to check your report regularly because ID thieves could target you at any time.

15. You should always be very careful about how you keep and dispose of anything with sensitive information on it. Do not just bin it or recycle it, make sure you shred it.

16. If a cash machine looks like it's been tampered with, use a different one.

17. Put your card away safely before you leave the cash machine.

If you ask for a receipt, take it with you to check it against your statement when it arrives and then dispose of it safely.

---

[i] Daily Mail Newspaper of 25th September, 2010
[ii] Jemma Smith from UK payments from Daily Mail Newspaper of 25th September, 2010

[iii] Daily Mail Newspaper of 25th September, 2010

[iv] Daily Mail newspaper of 11th August, 2010
[v] Daily Mail newspaper of 11th August, 2010
[vi] Daily Mail newspaper of 11th August, 2010
[vii] Metro newspaper of 18th October, 2010 by Tariq Tahir
[viii] Daily Mail newspaper of January 2007.